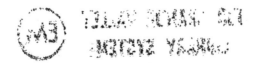

Science Experiments

FLIGHT

by
John Farndon

BENCHMARK BOOKS

MARSHALL CAVENDISH

NEW YORK

Marshall Cavendish Corporation

99 White Plains Road

Tarrytown, New York 10591

© Marshall Cavendish Corporation, 2002

Created by Brown Partworks Ltd

Library of Congress Cataloging-in-Publication Data

Farndon, John

    Flight / by John Farndon.
          p. cm. - (Science experiments)

Includes index.

Summary: Discusses the history of flight and suggest experiments to explore the
subject.

ISBN 0-7614-1342-1

    1. Aeronautics-Juvenile literature. 2. Flight-Juvenile literature. [1. Flight. 2.
    Flight-Experiments. 3. Aeronautics. 4. Aeronautics-Experiments. 5.
    Experiments.] I. Title. II Series.

TL547 .F372001

629.13-dc21   2001025214

Printed in Hong Kong

PHOTOGRAPHIC CREDITS

t – top; b – bottom; c – center; l – left; r – right

Corbis - p6, Joseph Sohm (b); p7, George Hall (tr); p10, Tom Brakefield
(b); p16, 17 Ted Streshinsky (b)
Hulton Getty - p4,5 (b); p5, (tr)
NASA - p17, (tr)
Pictor International - p12,13 (b)
Skyscan - title page, Chris Allan (c); p8, Ian Pillinger (br); p20, Chris
Allan(br); p25, Genevieve Leaper (tr); p28,29 Jon Davison (b)
Still Pictures - p11, B.Odeur (tr)
Tony Stone - p24,25 Joe McBride (b)
TRH Pictures - p13, (tr); p21, (tr); p29, (tr)

Step-by-step photography throughout: Martin Norris

Front cover: Martin Norris

Contents

TAKING OFF

Aircraft are the fastest means of transportation. They can soar straight over obstacles, such as mountains and oceans. Airliners (large passenger planes) can fly at over 500 mph (800 km/h). Some fighter planes can reach 2,000 mph (3,200 km/h). A trip across the Atlantic Ocean once took many days by sea. Now, it takes less than seven hours by air.

As a result, aircraft have transformed the way people travel. Millions of people now fly regularly far across continents

Did you know?

The first powered aircraft had a steam engine. The airplane was a large model made by Englishmen William Henson and John Stringfellow in 1845. It probably made one short flight.

In 1903, the Wright brothers' Flyer made the first controlled aircraft flight under power, at Kitty Hawk, North Carolina.

In the real world

FLYING MILESTONES

1909 Louis Blériot flies across the English Channel.

1914 The world's first regular air passenger service begins in Florida.

1919 John Alcock and Arthur Whitten Brown make the first nonstop flight across the Atlantic.

1927 Charles Lindbergh makes the first solo flight across the Atlantic.

1933 Wiley Post flies round the world.

1947 Chuck Yeager flies faster than sound in the Bell X-1.

1952 The *Comet* is the first jet airliner in regular service.

Amy Johnson was one of the great pioneering pilots of the 1930s, flying solo from London to Australia.

for short business trips and vacations. Major airports, such as Chicago's O'Hare, see scores of passenger flights every day.

People dreamed of flying for thousands of years. As long ago as the 15th century, Leonardo da Vinci (1452-1519) came up with an idea for an ornithopter, a machine with wings flapped by muscle power. But it was never made. Then, in the early 1800s, British engineer Sir George Cayley built the first glider, an aircraft with wings but no engine. It was not until 1903 that the American Wright brothers, Orville and Wilbur, made the first controlled flight in an aircraft that had an engine for taking off and powering it through the air.

LIGHTER THAN AIR

Hot-air ballooning is now a popular pastime. Flights last a couple of hours.

Airplanes rely on wings to lift them into the air, but the first successful flights were made without wings, in balloons. Balloons are lifted by a big bag of light gas. Because gas is lighter than air, the balloon floats up, just as a cork bobs up if you push it under water.

In 1783, the first balloon flights were made in France, in paper balloons made by the Montgolfier brothers. They filled the balloons with hot air

AIRSHIPS

The problem with balloons is that they simply float where the wind takes them. But in 1852, Frenchman Henri Giffard made a cigar-shaped gas balloon, powered it with a steam-driven propeller, and then added a rudder to make it "dirigible" (steerable). Later in the century, with petrol engines and rigid framed bags, dirigible balloons became airships—the first large aircraft. In the 1920s, large luxury airships carried people across the Atlantic in style. But a series of disastrous fires, caused by the inflammable hydrogen gas, made people realize that traveling by airships was far too dangerous.

The idea of airships was revived recently. The British-made Skyship is filled with helium gas, which is almost as light as hydrogen, but completely safe.

from a fire. Because hot air is less dense (lighter) than cool air, the balloons rose in the cooler air. One flight carried two men in a basket beneath.

A few months later, two other Frenchmen, Jacques Charles and M. Robert, made a different kind of balloon. They made a big bag from rubberized silk and filled it with hydrogen gas. Hydrogen is the lightest of all gases, so it lifted the balloon into the air.

Hydrogen-gas ballooning soon became popular because flights could last for several hours, unlike hot-air flights, which were over as soon as the air cooled. Gas balloonists could descend by using two control lines. One line let gas out through the top of the bag for going down. The other pulled open a "ripping seam" to let all the gas out once they were on the ground.

Hydrogen ballooning declined from 1900 when the first airplanes were made. People also realized how dangerous hydrogen is because it is inflammable, or likely to burst into flame. In the 1960s, however, Ed Yost, Tracy Barnes, and others in the U.S. began to experiment with hot-air balloons. Their balloons were made of nylon and filled with heated air made by burning propane gas from cylinders. The gas can be carried up with the balloon to replenish the hot air at any time. This proved so successful that hot-air ballooning is now a very popular hobby.

WARMING UP

You will need

- Two very large sheets of tissue paper
- A small hair dryer
- Paper glue
- Paper clips
- Scissors
- Cotton thread
- Thick paper or thin cardboard (for making the balloon basket)

1 Lay the sheets of tissue paper together and fold in half lengthways. Draw a half balloon shape and cut through both sheets together to make two matching balloon shapes.

In the real world

THE FIRST MANNED FLIGHT

Throughout 1782 and 1783, the French Montgolfier brothers experimented with paper hot-air balloons. On September 19, 1783, they sent a sheep, a duck, and a rooster aloft at the palace of Versailles, France, in front of an amazed King Louis XVI. Two months later, on November 21, two of Louis's courtiers, Pilatre de Rozier and François Laurent, became the world's first aeronauts. They went up in a Montgolfier balloon and sailed a distance of five miles (8 km) before landing safely in a field.

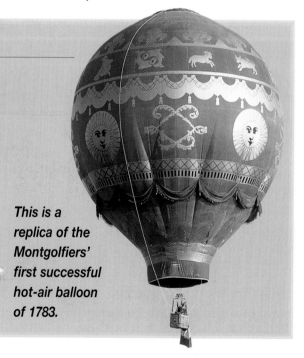

This is a replica of the Montgolfiers' first successful hot-air balloon of 1783.

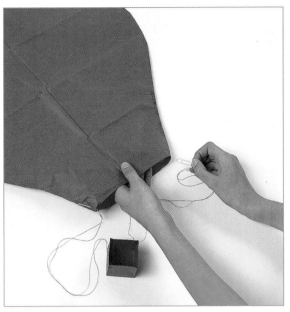

2 Glue the pieces together around the edge to make a bag, leaving a hole at one end. Make a basket as shown below. Glue thread to the edges of the basket then attach them to your balloon with paper clips.

To make the basket, cut out a shape like this from thick paper; fold up along the lines; and glue the tabs to make a cube.

Hold the top of the balloon with one hand, then fit the nozzle of a hair dryer, set at "low" heat, into the open end of the bag. Switch the hair dryer on and let the balloon fill with warm air. Keep holding on until you are sure it is full of really hot air. Now try letting go of the top of the balloon. With luck, it will float upward a little. This works best on a very cold day.

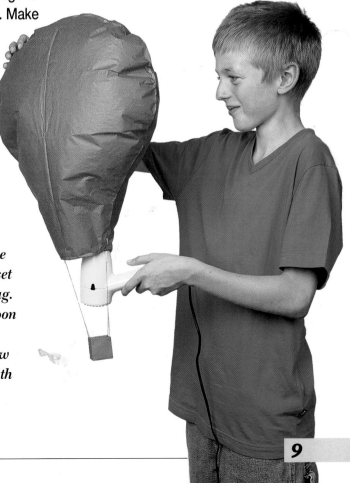

HOW BIRDS FLY

When landing, big birds like eagles raise their wings high and spread their tail feathers to act as brakes.

Birds are perfectly made for flying, with their wings and feathers and light, hollow bones. Birds usually fly using one of two main methods: either by gliding with their wings held still or by flapping their wings up and down.

Did you know?

Most birds fly between 20 and 60 mph (30–100 km/h). But the spine-tailed swift can fly at more than 100 mph (160 km/h), and the peregrine falcon can reach an astonishing 217 mph (350 km/h) when stooping (diving on its prey).

Gliding uses much less effort than flapping, and birds that are able to stay in the air a long time tend to be the best gliders. Only birds with long wings can glide well, because short wings do not give enough upward lift. Birds of prey, like kites, eagles, and falcons, are usually good gliders, hovering in the air as they search with their sharp eyes for food on the ground. So too are swifts, gulls, and gannets.

Many seabirds are good gliders, because they often have to fly long distances over the ocean without a rest. Albatrosses, petrels, and shearwaters have long narrow wings that enable them to soar upward on rising currents of warm air, called thermals. Often, birds circle upward on a thermal, then glide slowly down until they find another thermal to carry them up again. In this way, they can cover huge distances without once beating their wings. Albatrosses are especially good at this kind of gliding—called dynamic soaring—and can keep it up for many days on end.

Most smaller birds flap their wings to fly, and even birds that mostly glide flap their wings to take off and land. Powerful muscles in the bird's breast pull its wings up and down.

For the downstroke, one set of large feathers, called the

In the real world

Bats are the only mammals that can fly. A few others, such as flying squirrels, can glide a long way.

INSECT AND BATS

Birds are not the only creatures that can fly. Most insects have wings, too, and many can fly very well. Some insects, like flies and mosquitoes, have two wings. Dragonflies, bees, butterflies, and moths have four. Insects cannot glide like birds. Instead, most vibrate their wings so fast that they make a buzzing sound as they beat the air. Butterflies beat their wings four times a second; houseflies, 200 times; and midges, 1,000 times. The fastest flyers are dragonflies, which can reach 60 mph (100 km/h). Butterflies are slower, but they can fly 100 miles (160 km) without stopping.

primary feathers, close and push the air down and back. This thrusts the bird up and forward. For the upstroke, the primary feathers part and let air flow through as the wings gently rise, ready for another downstroke. Vultures flap slowly, while hummingbirds flap their wings so fast—sometimes more than 50 times a second—that the wings vanish into a blur.

FLYING ON WINGS

Unlike balloons, airplanes are heavier than air, but they can stay up because they have wings to support them. Wings provide the lift an airplane needs to get it into the air and to stop it from falling out of the sky.

Unlike bird and insect wings, airplane wings are completely rigid and do not flap or beat. But they work in a similar way to a bird's wing when the bird is gliding. The secret lies in the combination of the wing's movement through the air and its special shape.

A wing is not just long, thin and flat. It is very slightly arched from front to back, and it is also slightly fatter on the front or "leading" edge. If you took a

Jet airliners can fly on slim wings because they have powerful engines to push them swiftly through the air.

In focus

HOW WINGS WORK

An airplane's wing is lifted by air flowing above and beneath it as it slices through the air. Because the top of the wing is curved, air pushed over the wing speeds up and stretches out. This stretching of the air reduces its pressure. Underneath the wing, the reverse happens, and pressure here rises. The result is that the wing is both sucked up from above and pushed from below.

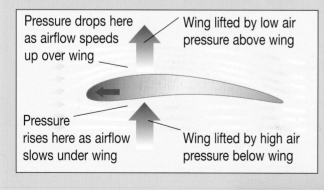

Pressure drops here as airflow speeds up over wing

Wing lifted by low air pressure above wing

Pressure rises here as airflow slows under wing

Wing lifted by high air pressure below wing

In the real world

WING SHAPES

In the early days of flying, wings were wide, rectangular, and stuck out almost at right angles to the body of the plane. But, as planes got faster and faster, wing shapes changed. Now, most jet-propelled planes have narrow, triangular wings swept back in a V. This shape cuts through the air more smoothly than a straight wing, allowing the plane to fly fast. Some fighters have "delta" wings that make a triangle down the entire length of the plane.

In fast flight, some fighter's wings swing right back toward the tail.

slice through an airplane wing, it would look a bit like a flattened comma.

A wing shaped like this is called an aerofoil. As an aerofoil slices through the air, it makes the air flow past it in such a way that the air flow lifts up the wing. How this happens is shown in the box on page 12.

Just how much lift the wing gives the airplane depends on the angle and shape of the wing and how fast it slips through the air. The shape of the wing is critical, and airplane makers spend a great deal of time designing it to provide just the right amount of lift.

Up to a point, the faster a plane flies or the more steeply the wing is angled, the more lift it provides. For instance, an airplane can get extra lift for climbing, by moving faster and dropping its tail end so that it cuts the air at a steeper angle.

AEROFOIL

You will need

✓ Several rectangular sheets of lightweight paper

1 Hold a piece of paper vertically between your finger and thumb, then let go. It will probably drop straight to the ground.

In the real world

WING MATERIALS

The wings of the earliest airplanes were made as light as possible. Typically, they were constructed of linen stretched over a thin wooden frame and stiffened with varnish. Although such wings were light, they were fragile, which limited how fast the airplane could fly. In the 1930s, airplane engineers began to design stronger wings of light metals, such as aluminum. These allowed airplanes to fly faster using more powerful engines. The extra speed and power produced more lift, so bigger, heavier planes could be built.

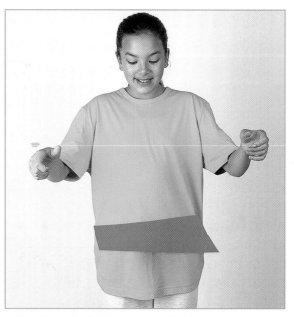

2 Now, hold the paper flat between your hands, as level as you can, then let go. It will flutter slowly to the ground.

What is happening?

All these experiments show how a wing is supported by air if it is the right shape and moves through the air in the right way. The last step shows how the real lift does not come from air pushing up the wing from underneath, but from the speeding up of air over the top. In your experiment, the wing is still, and the air is moving past it as you blow over the paper. The effect is the same when a wing moves through still air.

3 Next, grasp two corners of the paper's short edge and drag it swiftly through the air. The far end of the paper will lift.

Finally, grasp two corners of a shorter edge of the paper. Let the far end curve down loosely, so there is no stiffness in the paper. Now hold the edge of the paper up to your lips and try blowing across it. You might think it would be easier to lift the loose end of the paper by blowing underneath the paper to push it up. In fact, you will find it easier to lift the paper by blowing across the top. With practice, you should be able to get the paper to fly out almost level.

FLYING
FORWARD

Many modern jet airliners rely on four powerful turbofan engines to provide the enormous thrust that is needed to climb into the air.

An airplane's wings can only lift it when they are slicing through the air. So the plane must keep moving forward. If it ever stops moving or "stalls", the wings no longer give lift and the plane drops like a stone.

An airplane can keep moving just by falling gradually forward. Airplanes called gliders fly like this. But the plane slowly loses height, which is why glider flights are short. So most airplanes have engines. Engines provide the extra "thrust" or push to keep the plane moving forward. Engines also give the power for a plane to take off by itself and fly in any direction.

In the real world

SUPERSONIC FLIGHT

Supersonic aircraft fly faster than sound. Flying this fast, aircraft build up shock waves in the air that create a noise, or "sonic boom," that can be heard from the ground. A plane flying at the speed of sound is said to be at Mach 1. But because the speed of sound varies with height, Mach 1 is a different speed at different heights. At 40,000 feet, Mach 1 is 658 mph because the speed of sound at 40,000 feet is 658 mph. At 30,000 feet, Mach 1 is slower.

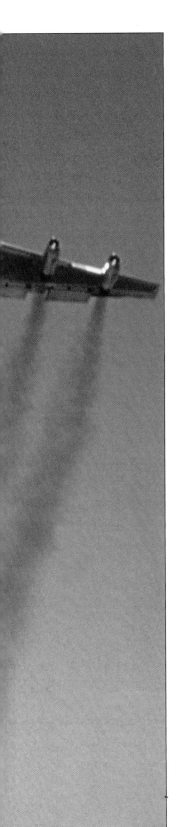

Scramjets like NASA's Hyper-X may one day reach 12,000 mph (19,200 km/h) in 7 seconds—and fly across the Atlantic in 20 minutes.

Airplane engines push or pull the airplane along in one of two ways. Small, light planes usually have engines similar to automobiles. The engine turns a propeller that pulls the aircraft through the air. A propeller has angled blades that act like spinning wings, thrusting the plane forward in much the same way as wings lift it upward.

Larger aircraft and most warplanes use jet engines. Jet engines are much more powerful than propeller engines and can thrust even big airliners along at speeds up to 1,200 mph (1,900 km/h)—almost twice the speed of sound.

The simplest jet engines, called turbojets, work by pushing a jet of hot air out the back to thrust the plane forward. Air is scooped in the front and squeezed by spinning blades, called compressors. The squeezed air is drawn into the middle of the engine. Here it mixes with a spray of fuel and is set alight. As the fuel and air mixture burns, it expands dramatically and bursts out the back of the engine as a high-speed jet of hot air that drives the aircraft rapidly forward.

Engines like these are used on the supersonic airliner, *Concorde*, and fast military planes. But most airliners use quieter and cheaper-to-run jet engines called turbofans. These combine the hot air jet with the backdraught from a whirling, multibladed fan to give the extra thrust needed at low speeds for take-off and ascent.

THRUST

You will need

- ✔ An empty toilet roll
- ✔ About 10 ft (3 m) of string
- ✔ Self-adhesive Velcro
- ✔ A balloon (long party balloons work best)
- ✔ Paints and a brush for decorating your train

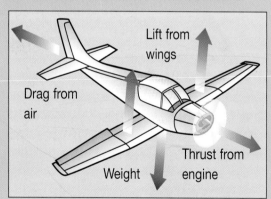

1 Paint a cardboard roll to look like a railway carriage. Stick two Velcro pads in line on the "underside" at either end.

In focus

FORCES ON AN AIRCRAFT

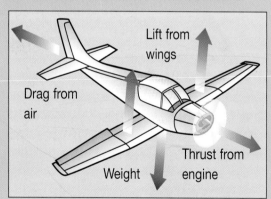

Lift from wings

Drag from air

Weight

Thrust from engine

The arrows in this picture show the direction of the four main forces acting on an aircraft: weight, lift, drag, and thrust.

Four main forces act on an aircraft when it is in the air. The aircraft's *weight* continually pulls it down toward the ground. The *lift* provided by the wings counteracts the weight and helps keep the aircraft aloft. The air around the plane rubs against it and provides a continual *drag* that holds the aircraft back. The engine (through either a propeller or a jet) provides the *thrust* to drive the plane forward, and so counteract the drag. Keeping the aircraft flying forward depends on keeping just the right balance between all of these four forces.

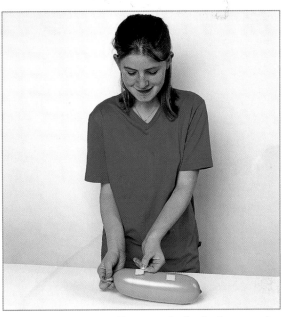

2 Thread string through your cardboard "carriage." Stretch the string across a room and secure at both ends.

3 Blow up a balloon and pinch the nozzle to keep air from escaping. With your other hand, stick on two pads of Velcro.

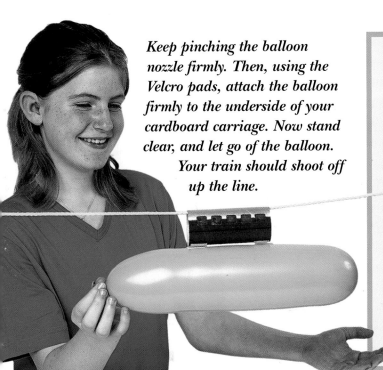

Keep pinching the balloon nozzle firmly. Then, using the Velcro pads, attach the balloon firmly to the underside of your cardboard carriage. Now stand clear, and let go of the balloon. Your train should shoot off up the line.

What is happening?

When you release the balloon, it quickly goes down as the stretchy rubber pushes out the air inside. As the air rushes out it collides with and pushes against the air outside.

This push is called thrust. The thrust provided by the air shooting from the balloon drives the balloon along the line. In the same way, aircraft rely on thrust to propel them through the air. A jet engine provides a similar kind of thrust, but relies on the rapid expansion of very hot gases, rather than the stretchiness of rubber.

BANKING AND DIVING

The Red Arrows acrobatic team have perfected the art of controlling a plane in the air and can put on spectacular formation flying displays.

Did you know?

In early planes, pilots sat in an open bay called the cockpit. Here they were exposed to howling winds, freezing cold and damp, with nothing more to protect them than a tiny windscreen. This is why most pilots wore warm clothes—wool-lined helmets and thick sheepskin coats, thick trousers and sheepskin boots.

A car can only be steered to the left or right, but an airplane can go up and down as well—and also roll from side to side. This is why controlling an airplane requires a good deal of skill and coordination.

Pilots talk about three kinds of movement in an airplane: rolling, yawing and pitching. Rolling is when the plane rolls to one side, dipping one wing or the other. Yawing is when the plane steers to the left or the right, like a car. Pitching is when the plane goes nose up or down to climb or dive.

All these moves are controlled by hinged flaps on the wings and tail (see below). By changing the angle of these flaps, the pilot redirects the airflow and so steers the plane.

To pitch up or down, the pilot in a manually controlled airplane pulls or pushes on a control stick. This raises or lowers the elevators.

To roll left, the pilot pushes the stick to the left. This raises the aileron on the left wing and lowers it on the right wing. To yaw left, the pilot pushes the foot-operated rudder with his left foot, swinging the rudder left.

In focus

CONTROL FLAPS
A plane is controlled in the air by moving hinged flaps on its wings and tail. There are three main kinds. Elevators are small flaps on the rear wings which control the pitch. Ailerons are large flaps on the main wings which control rolling. The rudder is a large vertical flap on the rear wing which controls yawing. Big jet arliners have additional flaps for giving extra lift for climbing, and others to act as brakes.

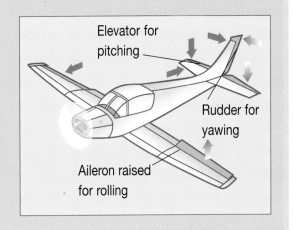

Elevator for pitching

Rudder for yawing

Aileron raised for rolling

CONTROL SURFACES

You will need

✓ Two rectangular sheets of lightweight cardboard (each in a different color)

✓ Paper clips

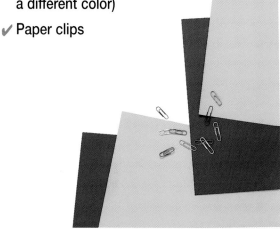

Making your plane

Work out your own way of folding paper to make an airplane, or follow these steps:

1. Fold paper in half then fold back a small triangle at one end of each half.

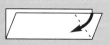

2. Fold another triangle back on each side from halfway along the top edge.

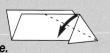

3. To make the wings, fold a triangle from halfway down the tail.

4. Open up the fold for wing triangles so they stick out at right angles.

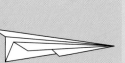

1 Fold a piece of paper in half lengthways, then make a paper airplane following the folding instructions on the left.

2 Fold down a small triangle at the end of the right hand wing as shown. Fold up a similar triangle on the left hand wing.

What is happening?

A well-designed ordinary paper airplane will fly straight and true for some way before veering off one way or the other. But these airplanes have extra folds that make them veer sharply to the left or the right. These folds act in exactly the same way as the ailerons (wing flaps) on a full-sized airplane, which make it roll to the left or right. When the right wing of your plane is folded upward, it reduces the lift on this wing and so makes the plane veer down to the right. When the left wing of your plane is folded upward, it reduces the lift on this wing and so makes the plane veer down to the left.

3 Now make an identical paper airplane, but reverse the flaps in step 2, with the right wing up and the left wing down.

Attach a couple of paper clips to the middle of the main fold for balance. Now grasp one of the paper airplanes firmly by the fold in the middle. Throw it as smoothly and firmly forward as you can. You will find it veers off sharply to one side. Now throw the other paper airplane in exactly the same way and in the same direction. You will find that this time it flies off in the opposite direction.

GLIDERS

Hang-gliders rely on catching rising air currents to sustain flights.

Gliders are airplanes without engines. They played a major role in the early days of flight, but interest in them declined for a while once the secret of powered flight was discovered.

Because gliders have no power, they can only fly "downhill." So in the early days, gliders could only stay in the air for a few seconds. Then in the 1920s, glider pilots found they could ride up on the wind

HOW A GLIDER IS LAUNCHED

Gliders can be launched into the air in several ways. Auto-towing means towing the glider along the ground behind an automobile until it is moving fast enough to climb high into the air. Winch-launches use a motor winch in the same way. Both methods are quick and cheap, but give only brief flights as the glider reaches a height of only 1,000 feet (300 m) or less.

For longer flights, gliders are often towed up into the air by a powered plane. This is known as an aero-tow.

rising over a ridge or hill. Soon after, they realized that even away from hills they could hitch a lift on thermals.

Thermals are rising currents of air warmed by the ground on sunny days. Skilled pilots soon learned to stay aloft for hours at a time and even make long cross country flights using thermals and other air currents as stepping stones. Now gliding is a popular sport.

Modern gliders are usually molded from GRP (glass reinforced plastic) to give a sleek, aerodynamic shape. An average one gives a glide ratio of 1:45. This means it will drop only one foot for every 45 feet it flies. Competition gliders give even better glide ratios.

GLIDER PIONEERS

In the early 1800s, Sir George Cayley (1773–1857) experimented with kites, and worked out how a wing works. In 1853, Cayley built the first full-sized glider, which, it is said, flew his terrified coachman across a valley. Soon, other pioneers were making longer glider flights, but the flights were erratic since no one knew how to control gliders in the air. Then in the 1890s German Otto Lilienthal, achieved control with a kind of hang-glider, by shifting his weight to change the wing angle. Sadly, he was killed during one flight, but his success inspired the Wright brothers.

MAKING A KITE

You will need

- ✓ An unused plastic garbage bag
- ✓ Adhesive tape
- ✓ String
- ✓ Scissors
- ✓ Paper clips
- ✓ Several bamboo skewers

1 Cut as large a flat rectangle as you can from the garbage bag and fold it as shown in the panel below.

Folding your kite

There are a huge number of ways of making a kite, and this is just a simple one. There are many more, including some so big they are able to carry a an adult aloft.

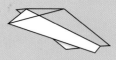

1. Fold the bag material carefully in half, then firmly press down the crease.

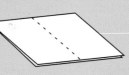

2. Draw a line from a point one third of the way along one side to two thirds along the far side.

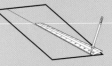

3. Fold back the bag material along your ruled line and press flat. You now have your basic kite.

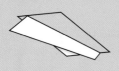

4. Turn the kite over then lift the fold line up and adjust until it is at right angles to the wing. Turn it back over.

Take your kite to a windy, open space. Unravel some string. Hold your kite aloft, and throw it up smoothly, holding on to the string. Then pull the string to drag your kite through the air, until it is caught on the wind. Gradually play out the string so that the kite is free to fly higher and higher.

2 Tape the bamboo skewers across the top of your kite to make the wing rigid.

3 Make a small hole in the underside fold of the kite and thread your string through it.

What is happening?

A kite is actually a wing. But rather than moving through the air like an airplane wing, it is held still by the string while the wind moves air past it. The wind pushes directly on the under side of the kite, keeping it taut on the string. But, as long as the kite is at the right angle to the wind, it will also act as an aerofoil to gain lift. Air flowing over the top of an aircraft wing drops in pressure and so sucks the wing upward. In the same way, the wind blowing over the top surface of the kite creates low pressure which sucks the kite upward.

HELICOPTERS

Helicopters are the most versatile of all aircraft. They can fly backward as well as forward. They can fly straight up and down or hover in the same place. And they can land in a space no bigger than a large truck.

The key to their versatility is the whirling rotor blades on top. The rotor blades are like very thin wings. As they whirl around, they cut through the air to provide lift, like the wings of an airplane. In this way, they haul the helicopter upward.

The rotor blades can also be slightly angled so that they act like a propeller and pull the helicopter along.

Besides the main rotor, a helicopter also has a small tail rotor. This pulls on the air to make sure it is the rotors that turn and not the whole helicopter instead. The tail rotor also acts as a rudder, and the pilot can change the pitch (angle) of its blades to allow the tail to swing to the left or right.

Helicopters take a great deal of skill to fly, because they have three main controls, not two as conventional aircraft have:

Small helicopters like this are used for anything from police surveillance to air taxi services.

Did you know?

Helicopters can lift enormous loads vertically. Some army helicopters can lift entire trucks straight off the ground. The Russian Mil Mi-12 Homer of 1968 could lift nearly 40 tons.

HELICOPTER RESCUE

The helicopter's ability to hover above the ground, or land in tiny spaces, makes it perfect for reaching dangerous or inaccessible places in an emergency. This is why helicopters are used by many rescue services. Many people trapped or injured in the sea or high on a mountain, owe their lives to a helicopter.

A helicopter winches an injured climber to safety.

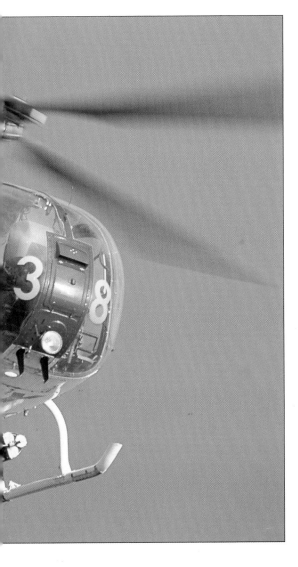

a "collective" pitch control, a "cyclic" pitch control, and, finally, a rudder that adjusts the tail rotor to steer the helicopter to the left or right.

To go up or down, the pilot uses the collective pitch control to alter the angle or pitch of the main rotor blades. When the blades cut through the air nearly level, they provide almost no lift. To climb, the pilot steepens the pitch to boost lift. To hover, the pilot sets a lower pitch. It all works through a sliding collar on the rotor shaft, called the swashplate, which pushes up or pulls down rods linked to the blades.

To fly forward or backward, or bank into a turn, the pilot uses the cyclic pitch control. The cyclic control mechanism is very complicated, but the effect is to tilt the whole rotor in the direction that the pilot wants to go.

Experiments in Science

Science is about knowledge: it is concerned with knowing and trying to understand the world around us. The word comes from the Latin word, *scire*, to know.

In the early 17th century, the great English thinker Francis Bacon suggested that the best way to learn about the world was not simply to think about it, but to go out and look for yourself—to make observations and try things out. Ever since then, scientists have tried to approach their work with a mixture of observation and experiment. Scientists insist that an idea or theory must be tested by observation and experiment before it is widely accepted.

All the experiments in this book have been tried before, and the theories behind them are widely accepted. But that is no reason why you should accept them. Once you have done all the experiments in this book, you will know that the ideas are true not because we have told you that they are but because you have seen for yourself.

All too often in science there is an external factor interfering with the result which the scientist just has not thought of. Sometimes this can make the experiment seem to work when it has not, as well as making it fail. One scientist conducted lots of demonstrations to show that a clever horse called Hans could count things and tap out the answer with his hoof. The horse was indeed clever, but later it was found that rather than counting, he was getting clues from tiny unconscious movements of the scientist's eyebrows.

This is why it is very important when conducting experiments to be as rigorous as you possibly can. The more casual you are, the more "eyebrow factors" you will let in. There will always be some things that you cannot control. But the more precise you are, the less these are likely to affect the outcome.

What went wrong?

However careful you are, your experiments may not work. If so, you should try to find out where you went wrong. Then repeat the experiment until you are absolutely sure you are doing everything right. Scientists learn as much, if not more, from experiments that go wrong as those that succeed. In 1929, Alexander Fleming discovered the first antibiotic drug, penicillin, when he noticed that a bacteria culture he was growing for an experiment had gone moldy—and that the mold seemed to kill the bacteria. A poor scientist would probably have thrown the moldy culture away. A good scientist is one who looks for alternative explanations for unexpected results.

Glossary

aileron: An aileron is a large hinged flap on the main wing of an aircraft. It pivots up or down to roll the plane to one side or the other. The aileron on the other wing pivots in the opposite direction at the same time.

aerofoil: A wing shape that provides lift. Typically it is curved down at the front and back and has a streamlined shape to help air flow over it easily.

banking: Banking is when a plane steers to the left or right and leans over in the direction it is turning, rather like a bicycle.

control surface: Control surfaces are hinged flaps that pivot to control an aircraft's movement through the air. Some, like ailerons and elevators, control the aircraft's direction. Others provide extra lift for take-off and climbing, or act as brakes for landing.

drag: Drag is the force that holds an aircraft back as it tries to fly forward. It is mainly air resistance: the friction between the plane and the air.

elevator: Elevators are small hinged flaps on the tail wings of an aircraft designed to direct the front of the plane upward or downward.

flap: See Control surface.

flight deck: The cabin at the front of the plane where the aircraft's crew sit at the controls.

glider: An aircraft that flies on fixed wings, but has no power of its own. It will fly only as long as it has sufficient height to glide down, or is lifted up by rising air currents.

joystick: Nickname for the control column used in the past by pilots to control the aircraft.

lift: The force that lifts an aircraft up and keeps it flying. Airplanes get their lift from the movement of the wings through the air.

pitch: The pitch is the angle an aircraft is flying through the air—that is, how much the nose is pointing up or down.

propulsion: The means used to drive an aircraft forward.

ramjet: A special kind of simple but noisy jet engine used in missiles to boost them to very high speeds.

rolling: Rolling is when the plane rolls to one side, dipping one wing or the other.

rudder: The hinged vertical flap on an aircraft's tail which steers it to the left or right.

thrust: The force pushing an aircraft forward through the air, usually provided by an engine.

turbojet: A jet engine which has a turbine (spinning fan blades) to make it quieter and more economical.

yawing: Yawing is when an aircraft steers to the left or the right like a car without banking.

Index